The Highland Game

CARNMORE LODGE SETTLEMENT, LETTEREWE WILDERNESS, WESTER ROSS.
This area where Carnmore Lodge lies is at the heart of the 70,000 acre Letterewe estate. Only accessible by boat or on foot, it is reputed to be the most remote house on the British mainland. To reach Carnmore by boat entails a six mile cruise down Fionn Loch, and I was lucky enough to do it on a beautifully sharp autumn day. After all my searches for the 'ideal' lodge location I reckon I found it here — it really does have dramatic atmosphere, in total isolation.

The Highland Game

LIFE ON SCOTTISH SPORTING ESTATES

Glyn Satterley

Introduction by Michael Wigan

SWAN·HILL
PRESS

ACKNOWLEDGEMENTS

Virtually all the photographs in this book portray and depend on the people in them, and without their participation there wouldn't be a book. So to all the models — thank you, and particularly for not looking at the camera, unless I'd asked.

Without the support, research, and insights of Michael Wigan this book would be by far the poorer. No matter how often I called him, or what I needed to know, he would always help. If he didn't know he pointed me to someone who would. Any seemingly closed doors he managed to open.

As mentioned in the Preface, Donny McKay was the inspiration for the whole project and I couldn't begin to repay him, Norma his wife, and daughter Kirstine, for all their friendship, help and hospitality.

Nor would the book exist without the huge contribution made by the multitude of keepers and ghillies. I'd like to mention especially Angus Ross of Achentoul, Dougie Russell of Letterewe, Jock Black of Inveraray, Alex and Farquhar Boyd of Kingie, Roddy McDonald formerly of Ben Armine, Ack Sutherland of Berriedale, Johnnie Hardie of Helmsdale, Angus Kennedy formerly of Borrobol, Sandy Reid of Blair Atholl, Alex MacDonald of Achnacarry, Gordon Beattie of Wyvis, the team of keepers at Invercauld — too many to mention by name, the North Harris estate keepers, and all at Reay Forest including Ian Morrison, Victor, Donald at Gober, Johnny Ross, Walter and Nigger, and Mark.

Throughout the ten years it took to produce the photographs I have been very dependant on the co-operation of the people who owned the estates. As I wanted to be as objective as possible, without any restrictions put on me, this was asking a lot, particularly as none of them knew me.

The following are a few of the owners to whom I am indebted, who allowed me to get on in my own way without interfering, and who gave me helpful suggestions, support and most generous hospitality: Lord Strathnaver, Capt. Farquharson of Invercauld, Capt. Freddie Wills of Coulin, Lord Thurso, Christopher Moran of Glenffidach, Mrs Panchaud of Tulchan, Mark Birbeck, Mr van Vlissingen of Letterewe, Sandy Stewart of Ardvorlich, Sir Donald Cameron of Locheil, His Grace the Duke of Atholl, and Her Grace Anne, Duchess of Westminster whom I will never be able to adequately repay for her generosity and enthusiasm.

I must also thank the many others, who have either helped me 'on the hill', befriended me, or contributed in some way with the production of this book, especially Geoffrey Churton, Alastair Simpson, John Charity, Mark Hughes, David Whitehouse, Robert Howden, the Woodley family, Martin Wills, Colin McKelvie, Alan Whitfield, Ezio Pallotta, Martin Naughton, the staff at Tulchan, and last but not least, Andrea my wife, whose input has been immense and encouragement never failing.

Copyright © 1992 by Glyn Satterley
Introduction © 1992 by Michael Wigan

First published in the UK in 1992 by Swan Hill Press an imprint of Airlife Publishing Ltd

British Library Cataloguing in Publication Data
A catalogue record for this book is available from the British Library

ISBN 1 85310 288 1

Printed by Livesey Limited, Shrewsbury

Swan Hill Press

An imprint of Airlife Publishing Limited, 101 Longden Road, Shrewsbury SY3 9EB.

PREFACE

I first became aware of the unique lifestyle of the Highland Sporting Estate while working on a previous book, *Life In Caithness & Sutherland*. I discovered that these vast Northern landscapes which had inspired me, and with which I felt such an empathy, were owned by only a few individuals and virtually the whole of the North comprised of estates: a stark contrast to the home counties where I had grown up. It was a chance meeting with Donny McKay, a gamekeeper from one of these Sutherland estates, which sparked my interest, and inspired a project which ten years on has resulted in this book.

What began as a look at 'A year in the life of a keeper', gradually developed into an exploration of an entire way of life. I discovered a lifestyle steeped in tradition, yet certain aspects of it were changing and disappearing, almost as quickly as I photographed them.

I met Donny through photographing a Sutherland postman at work. His house was routinely the last delivery of the day, and there was always a cup of tea waiting for the postie. From that brief meeting I was generously invited back anytime, and I went, as and when I could. We became friends and as well as learning a lot about the way of life from Donny's experiences and enthusiasm for his work, I went with him on whatever jobs he was doing at that particular time of the year. Even winter nights produced some action, either out on poaching patrol or looking for vermin. In early spring I was introduced to heather burning, and not just photographing it. I have fond memories of smokey lunches following a morning of strenuous flame-beating. Late spring and Donny was dealing with foxes. Early summer and I saw pointers patiently being trained, or reminded how to detect and indicate grouse, out on the moors. Most visits produced the odd drama; like the abortive attempt to remove a wildcat from the lodge toolshed; the chase that ensued after discovering the remnants of a poached deer by the roadside; or Donny's backside being attacked, a few paces in front of me by the farm collie. Those early experiences were invaluable to my understanding of the whole subject and I will be eternally grateful to Donny.

Gradually I made contacts on other estates, many due to Michael Wigan's research and inside knowledge, although it was still the world of keepers and ghillies which fascinated me. I loved the challenge of photographing them working in what were frequently horrendous weather conditions. On one occasion while winter hind-shooting with keeper Alex Boyd and his son Farquhar in Inverness-shire, it deteriorated to almost Arctic conditions and my hands became so cold I couldn't feel to focus. Farquhar had to break the ice on the loch in order to get us home with the boat load of hinds, and as we slowly made it back, heavy snow began to obliterate the landscape. I must admit I saw these keepers as rather heroic figures, out in the landscape battling against the odds and taking it all in their stride. They were reassuring to be out on the hill with, extremely knowledgeable about their environment, and great company. For my part I feel it is important to muck-in, whatever the situation, and be yourself, rather than being a photographer demanding special consideration.

During the time spent observing keepers at work, I couldn't help but notice the unique relationship between the estate owner and his keeper or ghillie. On the hill the keeper as stalker is very much the boss. On the grouse moor the keeper plans and dictates the day, and on the river the ghillie 'suggests' what fly to use and where to fish. Yet tradition dictates that they eat their packed lunches at a suitable distance from each other. As my experiences and contacts widened, I began to have a greater understanding of the rules of the game and the ability to come to terms with them visually.

I became a regular visitor on many estates, and felt equally at home photographing the owners and their guests, as I did the estate employees. One situation led to another. The owner or guests at one lodge would say 'Have you been to North Harris? The ghillies carry the stags home on their backs there, since it is too steep for ponies' or 'Did you know they had a piper playing round the dinner table at Invercauld?' If I was interested, an introduction was kindly arranged for me, so I am indebted to a number of people for these invaluable tip-offs.

In this way I was invited to photograph in a great variety of estate lodges, sharing grand twelfth of August dinners, ghillies' balls, and occasionally being treated like royalty. I was accepted into many situations I would never otherwise have been given access to, certainly not socially. However it was as important for me to communicate the atmosphere inside the Duchess of Westminster's lodge at the ghillies' ball, as it was to capture the bizarre excitement of foxing at midnight in the middle of a moor.

My view of this way of life has always been that of the enthusiastic observer, not as a hunting, shooting, or fishing enthusiast. As a photographer I was curious to see and understand a lifestyle I found fascinating. Since previous presentations of sporting estates had come from Victorian sporting artists, a view very much from the inside, and few, if any, contemporary presentations exist, I felt it was a challenge to try and portray it today. I have tried to be as objective as possible in dealing with all issues, whether I agreed or disagreed, liked or hated. I photographed what I saw, how I saw it.

I still have difficulty coming to terms with the idea of killing for sport, but I do appreciate the lure of the Highland arena, and the uniqueness of the life it encompasses.

Glyn Satterley

THE PRACTICE TARGET, SUISGILL, SUTHERLAND.
These functional sculptures can be seen on most deer forests, many created by Victorian craftsmen. In spite of having withstood many years of 'abuse', this one still works beautifully as a silhouette. I've seen it fool even experienced stalkers, as they come upon it, on their way to the hill.

6

INTRODUCTION
by Michael Wigan, author of *The Scottish Highland Estate*

*T*he Highlands is a much talked about place. To outsiders it is thought of as a single sea-girt mountainous area, noted for its beauty, and violent romantic history, and rain. To its inhabitants and those who pilgrimage north annually for summer holidays the term Scottish Highlands embraces several profoundly different regions, not so dissimilar in appearance, but quite different in character, and certainly to be distinguished from the rest of Scotland. Thus a Sutherland game keeper on referring to a certain person as being 'from the south' was corrected 'No, he's from Perth'. 'That's what I said' persisted this 'north man' as northern newspapers call locals, 'he's fae the sooth'. Highlanders may pride themselves on regional differences but one thing that welds disparate parts of the Highlands together is the form of land use, the one celebrated in this book.

Over most of the land area the Highlands is used and managed for country sports. Where the land has been converted to another use, for example forestry, sporting use is relegated to a by-product, and where, as in Orkney, most of the land has been turned to agricultural use, nature has been kind and provided in compensation wonderful loch fishing and wild-fowling. It may seem a grand claim but a sporting person can keep himself actively amused in one way or another over most of the year over most of the Highlands. The earliest salmon rivers open in January, at which time the season for shooting red deer hinds is not yet completed; in spring, summer and autumn the sportsman is spoilt for choice.

This munificence of sporting opportunity puts the Scottish Highlands into a separate category from most of Britain and Europe. The result is an indigenous population well versed in country lore, the intricacies of natural variety, and familiar equally with rod and gun. Try opening a conversation about trout fishing in a country bar anywhere north of the Highland line and you will see what I mean. The love of country sports goes back a long way into the old Gaelic culture, and when King David established his royal hunting forests in the 1130s the twin management policies of conservation of game and game habitat were well understood by a society imbued with the hunting spirit.

The establishment of the sporting estate, emulating the enthusiasm of Queen Victoria and Prince Albert at Balmoral, is often cited as the start of land management for deer, the animal that has existed alongside man for the longest time and has been utilised by him most consistently. Scientists have now found that not only were deer managed by man in the Highlands long before the Victorians, but long before the early medieval hunting forests too. A study of bones and artefacts reveals that at the end of the Ice Age deer were being culled selectively, intrinsically a policy of control and conservation. In the warming environment, with the growth of scrub birch and pine, red deer proliferated, replacing the reindeer of the earlier tundra. There is evidence to show scrub was burnt, as heather is now, to provide fresh shoots for deer to eat. Winter feeding of deer, hailed by some as an unnatural innovation on deer forests in the 1980s, actually began thousands of years earlier. By 15,000BC it is thought that husbandry of deer may have been as important an activity as random food gathering.

The earliest written evidence of hunting's codes of practice shows a thought-out, detailed and environmentally-sensitive awareness. The main elements of policy in King David's numerous hunting reserves were similar to aims today: prevention of poaching, protection of habitat (woodland then, heather today) and restriction of pasturage (mostly pig-range then, and sheep-range today). From the earliest times the possession of hunting rights — the first property rights in Scotland — were twinned with the obligation to protect habitat. So keenly was protection of habitat regarded that by 1535 the death penalty was in use for third-time wood-cutting offenders. To compensate the common people for restrictions imposed in the hunting forest control over lesser game, such as rabbits, was given over to them.

Humanitarian concerns were equally advanced, and mirroring present day wild-fowling bans in hard weather, hunting deer in snow storms was forbidden by the 15th century; so too was hunting hares in snow. Falconry propagated Britain's first protection laws for raptors, with draconian punishments for offenders introduced by James III of Scotland in 1474. Again, humanitarian regulations were intricate. Game birds (partridges, duck, plover, blackcock) could not be killed while moulting, a restriction which also applied to cranes and herons. Sharp practices were obliterated from recreational hunting methods, fair play and love of sport infusing the entire chivalric ideals. During one period, if a hare eluded the hounds for long enough the dogs were called off. When sheep were introduced into straths and glens in the early 19th century, in the precipitate introduction of a completely new land-use, one of the most resented impacts was partial disappearance of the game animals from which the Highlanders had stocked their larders. This sentiment persists today in a quite different situation, as evinced by the light sentences passed in local court-rooms on poachers chasing deer or salmon.

It is the volume of chronicling, both with pen and paint brush, that marked out the Victorian era as the Highland field sports era above all others. Indeed in those days the sheer scale of the human migration northwards for the sporting 'season' was awesome. The fact that transport was limited augments the impression, created by the Victorian artist George Earl, that the bulk of high society thronged Euston Station's platform to get to Scotland by the Glorious Twelfth. Numbers of sporting visitors were invariably outweighed by the seasonal staff imported, and gathered locally, to cater to their every whim. At Balmoral under Queen Victoria one retinue of servants was brought with her from England and encountered, with surprise registering on both sides, her resident staff of Highlanders. They dined and were billeted separately. This did not stop one Highlander opining the English were inclined to consume too much from the beer barrels which lined the wall, a judgement pronounced despite the fact that at this time the stalkers' and ghillies' special 'whisky money' equated with a bottle of the hard stuff per day!

What the Highlands inspired in the Victorian sportsman is still, essentially, the response evoked today. The early Victorian enthusiasts had the extra thrill of coming on a scene in the process of rapid adaptation. The leases of sporting properties were being drawn up swiftly, for widely differing rents, referring to areas of ground which were often dimly defined. Their financial resources gave these adventurers the run of a beautiful country abounding with game where, for a relative pittance, they could enjoy sporting pleasures to their hearts' content. The thrill of the sporting encounter itself remains the same, but the early pioneers enjoyed huge spaces in which to seek variety. The sporting tour, such as that described by the Yorkshireman Colonel Thomas Thornton in 1786, must have been an undertaking of unbounded enjoyment and interest. Thornton describes covering huge tracks of the Highlands at a time when conveyance was by boat, or horse and gig on rough tracks. Everywhere he went he secured willing ghillies, boatmen and guides keen to help satiate his hunger for fishing, shooting and falconry.

The land seen through Thornton's eyes was a veritable arcadia. Scotland's physical beauty rose to its best; delicious wild berries lined the highways, and freshness made the air intoxicating. A day of modest sporting success was followed by bumper catches or bags, and a reminder of the Highlands' natural bounty. There were, admittedly, disappointments — the inn at Ballindalloch lacked eggs, porter, brandy, rum, hay or corn for his horse, and windows — but generally his pen's admiration was only curbed when emerging from the Highland communities onto the coast. He noted that Highland ladies danced more keenly than in the south, and the lairds' tables, to which his good connections in England gave him access, were heaped with fresh fish and game and good drink. Undismayed by the inevitable bad weather days, Thornton's only real grievance was the exorbitant fee now and then demanded by a boatman or ghillie. Yorkshire tight-fistedness, or Highlanders sensing the golden opportunity?

I am only 40 but I can recall in my early teens a quasi-Edwardian scene in the house I now live in, a shooting lodge in Sutherland called Borrobol. My grandmother was then the matriarch, and the house was run like a sporting hotel, except that the guests were friends rather than clients. From August and through the shooting and stalking season until late October house parties routinely numbered about six. I remember as a small boy noting that the number of domestic staff roughly equalled the number of guests. There were pantry maids, house maids, cook and assistant cook. The back end of the lodge was a flurry of footsteps and an aviary of chatter; the main half was entombed in a more sombre atmosphere. Or so it seemed to a teenager who joined the ranks of dinner-jacketed personages in the smoking room before eight. My grandmother's ice-blue eyes scanned my apparel on entry into the room. I was required to name the pools I had fished, flies employed, along with procedural narrative (maybe the reason why, to this day, my grip on the names of fishing pools is horribly weak). As I graduated to stalking so I had to report every manoeuvre in the day, changes of wind, movement of stags, description of stags, and all the circumstantial detail of the shot. Rather to my surprise I find myself now, from her chair, making the same enquiries of my guests.

As my grandmother herself excelled at the activities she practised, she saw no reason why my sister too should not follow suit. My sister was despatched with the estate ghillie to learn fishing. When they arrived on the river bank my sister produced a book, explaining she had no interest in fishing; he was to use the rod. Impressed by the number of fish stacking up in the larder my grandmother decided at the end of the week to come down to the water and witness my sister's striking progress. My sister and her co-conspirator exchanged a desperate look . . .

My grandmother herself epitomised the approach of an earlier generation. Although a keen stalker she only took up fishing as a full time occupation after her husband's demise. She then fished the best part of five months every year on the Helmsdale until she was in her late 70s. During her last twenty-odd fishing years, for which her ghillie has documented records, she caught over 6,000 fish, in the process becoming a local legend. Her routine was iron-clad. She fished the same hours every day from 9.30 until tea, irrespective of weather, or conditions. She fished a line that was unfailingly straight. If the wind got stronger the line whipped out, if anything, straighter. If it reached gale force she undercut it, forever ruler-like. The angle of cast was just as systematic. Her rod tip, against modern fashion, was held high. Her concentration seemed never to waver. She walked between pools at a pace that would have been extraordinary in a man, a pace which, in fact, often unmanned men. She was, it must be said, extremely competitive, and if the other rod had by any stroke of fortune caught more fish by lunchtime she was not unduly pleased. The scores were almost invariably reversed after lunch. My grandmother, as they say, knew fish. In another particular too she was very much of her time: she always fished with a ghillie. This lady who had emptied so many salmon from the river never tied on her own fly.

I started fishing for salmon in August, in her lunch break. The ghillie put me on the pool and left. He remembers lunch on the river bank being interrupted when this little figure wearing a kilt with wellingtons underneath came running up saying 'Johnny, I'm stuck, I'm stuck'. When we returned to the pool I picked up the rod and the rock on which I had stuck began to move and swim downstream. My grandmother decided I would be a lucky fisher (she was very superstitious), a reckoning I have not always had reason to agree with.

Fishermen tell tales because a lot happens on rivers. The act of fishing promotes incidents. Those stories about hooking a cow or a sheep on the back cast, and having to snip the line as they race away, are likely to be right, because flicking a flying steel hook through the air is an act with many potentialities. I have seen a bat hooked on the back cast, at first glance a rare contingency until you consider the parallel habits and habitats of sea-trout fishers and bats sharing the gloaming. Of course the big fish are the ones that get away: that is how they grow big, by surviving. Also there is a limit, with a fly rod, to the amount of purchase an ordinary mortal can put on a salmon in fast water. Big fish do not play by the rules: they play survival sense. On the Spey they call it 'ottering' when a large salmon lies across the current, pointing slightly down stream, to put maximum pressure on your tackle and break free.

Naturally, close relationships are formed between ghillies and gamekeepers and those they take to river and hill. The sportsman in front of his ghillie or stalker is without his protective social carapace. If you play a big fish for 20 minutes at the close of a week in which little has happened, emotions are running high. No one can hide the feelings of triumph or disappointment which follow a particularly tricky stalk or a fish which has been testing to land. It is the ones you lose and which get away which often stay in the memory longest. In a sense nothing really separates the guide and the guided in achieving a good catch or a good stalk. I discovered this stalking as a boy in Sutherland with a stalker who was a renowned shot. We had one stag and were coming home when down a slope beneath us we saw a beast absent-mindedly gazing across the flats. To my surprise the stalker instructed me to crawl in a bit. The stag was a long way off. I was shooting with open sights and the ball nestling in the V of the end-sight blotted out the front half of the stag completely. To my anxieties the stalker replied, 'he's a dead stag'. And so it was. In the psychological sense the boy of 15 did not make the shot, the stalker did.

This is perhaps one reason why many of those who have fished or stalked a lot are just as happy ghillieing or stalking for someone else. To these people it is always more testing to help get success for someone else than to achieve it themselves. Stalkers and ghillies who keep immaculate records of days spent with their charges, annotating each fish caught or deer shot, sometimes have leaner records of the exploits they performed themselves. It has been remarked that only when at play is man really himself. Ghillies and stalkers know the intimate side of those with whom they spend their professional lives better than many of these people's customary company. Deep bonds of friendship and respect can develop over the years, a reality little surmised by those who casually dismiss the keepering and ghillieing professions as subservient. The truth is the other way around; ghillies and stalkers are the real masters of all they survey.

What is special about Highland sport? What is the muse that draws the southern entourages northwards every summer as powerfully now as ever? Listen to the old chronicler Sir Montague Fowler writing about a day on Braemore:

'Is there any sport — at least in the British Isles — which is comparable to deer stalking? I know of none in which all the resources of mind and body are called into play, and none in which the day's enjoyment is equally great whether or not a shot is fired. It is 50 years since I killed my first stag, and yet there is always a novelty of environment, a difference of tactics, a new experience, with each successive stalk. The hills are the same, the deer are the same, the weather is . . . the same, and yet, from beginning to end of the day, the conditions and happenings are dissimilar to anything of which one had previous cognition . . .

'On arriving at the beat one at once commences to spy the ground. This is a process which must not be hurried. Every inch of the hillside must be examined, and sometimes one will only discover a stag, which is comfortably lying in a peat bog, by a momentary flash of the tips of his horns as he lifts his head. Perhaps there are several herds in sight, in each of which there may be one or more stags worth a shot . . . We have now decided which stag to stalk, and it will mean a long climb over the top in order to get round and above them. But before we can disappear from their sight there is a piece of bare ground — a distance of about 100 yards — which must be traversed. At once we fall on hands and knees, crawling slowly. Even now there is a small knoll to be surmounted, and here we are in danger of being seen. So we lower ourselves, and for 25 yards we wriggle along like snakes — heedless of the fact that we are going through moist peat and pools of water — until we are behind the ridge, and safely out of sight. As we rise and shake ourselves we realise that we are soaked to the skin, and our clothes have taken a darker hue from the peat.

'Now follows a long strenuous climb. Suddenly the stalker, who is just in front of me, stops dead and drops to his knees. I instantly do the same. What has happened? Just in front of us, within 40 yards a hind and calf are feeding. Slowly we raise our heads, to find her staring at us. What has made her suspicious? Surely she could not have seen us? No, but as I dropped down my boot struck a rock with a slight noise, and her acute sense of hearing told her something was wrong.'

The day proceeds, by fits and starts, to a satisfactory conclusion. Sir Montague closes like this:

'I know of few experiences, in the recreative side of life, which give one a greater feeling of self-satisfaction or create a keener sense of goodwill towards the world in general, than to return home in the evening, having got two good stags, killed instantaneously. One has given evidence of skill in stalking, of perseverance, of accurate marksmanship; and at the same time one has replenished the larder . . . '

A stalking day is full of incidents and obstacles. Weather, wind and light are prone to change, throwing the whole strategy into fresh perspectives. Deer move and change position, get up to feed, lie down to rest, or trundle on their inscrutable courses over the skyline. There are the other denizens of moorland to contend with, a flurry of ptarmigan flushing from the rocky scree and alerting the quarry, or an alarmed grouse getting up with piercingly vocal consternation. It is not so long ago that on some stalking-only properties keepers were given orders to stamp on any grouse eggs they found, to prevent disruptions to stalking! The wealth of incidents and scope for mishap are encapsulated in a game book entry I came across at Ben Damph. 'October 10. Hughie broke the ponies' traces, lost a salmon, and shot his binoculars'. Of all the unpredictable elements, people come high on the list. Once at Borrobol the stalker and rifle had made a heroic crawl over flat country. The stalker asked the rifle, a continental hunter, to get in position. Feeling something heavy on his head he peered round to find the client neither to left or right but behind, pushing the rifle forward on the most available rest — his deer-stalker bonnet.

Stalking not only changes with the vagaries of weather, it changes with the seasons. In August, generally the earliest month in which stags are shot in Scotland, deer are in large parties, especially stags. Once on Borrobol I saw two parties of stags of 500 and 300 moving slowly up a hillside in late July cropping grass and heather as they went. I have read of even larger parties being seen in the central Highlands, stags building up their weight and condition before the rut moving forward seeking fresh ground. The next time stags are in big concentrations is when they assemble into winter groups and crop the hill mosses in November. Large parties are difficult to stalk. Their progress when cropping and walking is deceptively fast. Those stalkers who have been lucky enough to intercept them feeding in this way will never forget the thrill of being tucked out of sight as the mighty procession flows by.

The rut breaks in late September and the character of life amongst the deer completely alters. In forests with good numbers of stags the big master-stags can be seen making great efforts to herd and chivvy their unmanageable harems of hinds. Smaller stags break into the forbidden territory, particularly at night, and other large stags appear from far away regions to lodge a challenge. Watching fighting stags is one of the thrills of being on the hill in the rut. Some adroit stalkers can pull stags towards you by making guttural grunts and roars. The surprising thing is how ready stags are to challenge, how unquestioning their hormone-driven aggression and dominance drive. I have seen the most improbable of roars result in them trotting straight over. The general melee, to an all-night deep-throated orchestration, makes the unexpected commonplace. Exhausted stags, or those worsted in battle, can jump out of peat-hags as you almost walk on top of them; stags can appear at your back challenging stags in your front; stags in the latter phases of exhaustion in the rut plod muddle-headedly in a semi-conscious daze. Stalkers find themselves the opportunists of circumstance rather than the architects.

Such is the nature of stalking that funny things happen, things which if you invented them would not be believed. My grandfather, Sir Iain Colquhoun, stalking on a hot day took off his shirt before gralloching the stag and hung it on the prostrate beast's antlers. As he drew his knife the stag suddenly flickered its eyelids, jumped up, and ran off with the shirt flapping on its head. The bullet instead of killing had grazed it, causing it to lie down stunned. My stalker and I had the same experience — although we remained fully-clad — with a marauding stag shot through the horizontal wires of a deer fence. The stag dropped like a stone and the stalker was actually bending over it when it leapt to its feet and high-tailed off without stopping, across a river and over a far-off ridge. We watched it all the way with binoculars and undoubtedly it was unmarked. A bullet flying over the spine can have this effect, or one passing in front of the chest. This time the shot must have been deflected by a wire.

I once lost a stag which was under my feet. It happened like this. I was invited to stalk on a neighbouring forest and I shot one stag from a party after which my host shot another. We saw them unmistakeably drop dead. We gralloched my stag and walked over to where the other had fallen. Nothing was there. A three-quarter hour search ensued in which all the nearby ground, and even the neighbouring estate's closest glen, was repeatedly scanned for a wounded beast. The three of us returned forlornly to where we had started. I noticed the heather dipping away slightly below us. The stalker probed with his stick which vanished into a hole in the ground. On all fours we discovered a plug-hole deep in the peat, about the height of a room; at the bottom lay the stag. The stalker's face took on a dubious expression. He would have to go down, gralloch the stag in the cavern and somehow get it near

enough to the surface for us to grip it. Pulling a fifteen stone stag vertically upwards from below your feet is no mean achievement; the fact that none of us could stop laughing did not help. But the cardinal rule was observed: we got the stag home.

Before the days of all-terrain vehicles there were large parts of many forests that could not be reached and were known as deer sanctuaries. One day long ago a stalker on Borrobol had out with him a guest determined to get a certain stag which strayed, as they stalked it, into the sanctuary, a large level area of deep peat banks and sodden mossy tundra. The resolute guest said, yes, he wanted to get the stag at all costs. Which he did. Then came the dragging of it. This experience has to be endured to be understood. Heaving a dead weight over this sort of country can deflate the fittest athlete. The rifle asked the stalker what the venison value of the stag was, and on being told offered to pay as much provided they could leave the wretched burden behind. Of course, no Highland stalker would have any of such a plan and the two of them laboured on painfully until they reached the pony. As the stalker remarked, 'the gentleman never shot a stag in the sanctuary after that'.

Much of stalking's enjoyment comes later, in recollection. A day on the hill does not end when you get home to tea, it ends when you nod off weary in body and happy in spirit, thinking of the wild country where you have spent the day. Asked by a lady where and when he had had his most 'particular' stalk the old Glenfeshie stalker John Ferguson replied 'in bed where I recall the day's work and ask myself where I blundered, and profit accordingly when next on the hill'. The late Sir Iain Colquhoun described the end of an arduous but successful day with two stalking parties as follows:

'Down to the bothy Hughie and I go. The stove is lit and soon our soaking kilts are steaming before the fire. An hour more and we are sitting down to as fine a supper, cooked by ourselves, as the heart of man could require. Pipes were lit and the chairs drawn up to the stove. That wonderful hour had arrived — the rich reward of the man not afraid to spend every ounce of his strength when called upon to do so. Tired muscles relax and a sense of splendid physical well-being flows over and envelopes one like a rich warm tide. The story of each of the trophies hanging on the wall is told and retold. The old Scots songs are sung. Lastly Hughie tunes the great Highland war pipes and they change hands again and again until far into the night . . . We roll ourselves in our plaids; in five minutes no sound disturbs the silence of the hut save the gentle lapping of the water on the shores of the loch. The myriad sounds of the night blend into one sweet soothing noise.'

Stalking is indeed a life and death business. In going onto the hill not only is the stalking party entering an ancient, depopulated domain, once the home to thousands of subsistence farmers, but it is in an area redolent with the stalking toils and travails of hundreds of years. Most sports have their classic cautionary tales, narratives which make one pause for thought, and stalking is no exception. Only a short time ago a titled young Scotsman out stalking fell on his rifle and killed himself by accident, a simple tragedy made more complex when the poor man's family realised that a hundred years earlier his ancestor, bearing the same title, did the same thing; and it happened on the same deer forest. Aside from coincidences and calamities there is an inescapable haunting quality to stalking obvious to any who have done it.

Modern stalking has not changed in the fundamentals, but new philosophies now surround red deer control and the responsibilities of stewardship. Not very long ago the hind cull was undertaken as an occasional exercise, procuring venison for the larder and levelling numbers after the cull of stags in a leisurely way. Hind culling in the 1990s has become a major operation, particularly for those estates in the East Highlands where populations, after several mild winters, have grown too big. Now, come rain or shine, on many estates each day of the long hind season is a valuable one, and numbers of hinds to be removed have risen in some cases to three times historic figures. This has provided opportunities for stalking enthusiasts unable to afford stag-season rents, and is in the process of extending the sporting season in the Highlands right up through Christmas and after New Year. Where there is extreme pressure on numbers of hinds to be shot stalkers find guests a hindrance, and prefer taking their own rifle, selecting hinds through the telescope and firing as they move through the group. But for young tyros able to secure hind stalking a better introduction to the craft could not be found.

In many ways the hinds require a greater range of skills than the stags. The day is shorter and harsher; looming dusk is forever propelling the action forward. Temperatures are lower than in the autumn, winds possibly stronger, light worse, ground wetter. Not infrequently it gets so cold that by holding your binoculars in front of your eyes the warmth condenses on them and they mist up. You may have to suck your trigger-finger to restore its sensibilities.

The hinds are a harder target. The slightly smaller body size makes no appreciable difference but the hinds greater alertness, sense of self-preservation and protection, combined with the season coinciding with the peak of the animal's fitness, makes the hind a tougher stalking proposition. A hind which is suspicious remains on danger alert whereas a stag often re-settles. Hinds are in well-organised female groups with leaders, look-outs and watches posted on all sides. Movement into the firing position needs to be slower and more careful, and more of the stalker must remain concealed. (An old Rothiemurcus stalker used his long beard as camouflage, pushing it up in front of him when on the firing-bank). The only advantage the hind shooter has over the hunter of stags is that hinds' social cohesiveness means that sometimes individuals hang back after a key hind has been shot. Probably they are younger relations. Hind shooting not only calls for individual selection and the ability to tell old and infertile beasts from young breeders, a judgement which can only be refined by experience, but it also demands the ability to stay cool as beasts mill about, and make a succession of accurate shots. On occasion there is the unpleasant necessity of shooting dependent calves. It is only recently that estates arriving on the property market have quoted numbers of hinds shot, but the fact that this has become standard shows that the regard in which hind shooting is held, and its sporting value, are adjusting to modern conditions.

Stalking has always for me been the quintessential Highland sport, partly because open-hill stalking takes place nowhere else, and more particularly because it has a seriousness of purpose which universally affects those who have done it. The red deer is a keynote mammal in European culture and once served as the source of all the necessities of life. Deer horns split the stones of the first neolithic monuments; antler picks mined for flint to make man's first heavy tools. To shoot one of these well-proportioned, delicate, beautifully camouflaged and adapted animals is a serious business which gives rise in the rifle to thoughts of his own impermanence and tenuous adherence to life. Set against some of the most beautiful scenery anywhere, in one of the world's oldest and most weathered mountain ranges, which was once the height of the Alps, these intimations of mortality can reach a pitch of almost painful acuteness. The hills are eternal, and man is fiery and fit for a brief time. For this complex mix of reasons, added to contemporary man's distance from many realities of nature, people who stalk for the first time frequently return in a state of intoxicated fulfilment, a transformation surprising no-one more than themselves. From a new generation of hind stalkers will come greater familiarity with our grandest wild mammals, referred to affectionately by the Victorians as the 'moss-troopers'.

It sometimes surprises me that fishing is the sport that has surged in popularity in recent years. Ninety per cent of the action is out of human view; most of the time you appear no closer or further from your goal but to be getting and going nowhere; the physical action is repetitive; the whole endeavour remarkably solemn and unproductive. All of these things bring the imagination into play. How many times has it been remarked, 'The fish came just when I wasn't concentrating'. If thoughts could govern the world, as the Tibetan Buddhists believe, affairs would be run from the riverbank, where thinking runs deep. Truly river and loch are soothing places, carrying away on their ceaselessly replenished waters much human sorrow and stress. Extreme concentration works its restorative purposes just as well as extreme reverie. Where the archetypal stalker is sardonic and taciturn, the archetypal fishing ghillie is quick-witted and quick-tongued. It is worth pondering why it is that of all those ghillies who have spent their lives on the riverbank, usually the same riverbank, you seldom meet a dull, shallow, or superficial character. The water has worked for many hours to mould these men; and of course they have seen many people from different walks of life, and that can have a sobering effect too.

I once wrote up a ghillieing story about unsobriety. On a river which must remain unnamed the rods appeared at start of fishing to await the arrival of the tardy ghillie. A boat came round the corner spinning in the current, a few extremities of the ghillie visibly poking over the gunwale. The prostrated inebriate floated through several busy beats before being hauled ashore. The man was dismissed. I chronicled the tale as told, mentioning that the supine ghillie possessed a red beard. Shortly after an affronted letter arrived from the relevant estate office protesting at my story and saying the new ghillie on the beat was getting unwelcome publicity from it as he also had a red beard. Well, fishing stories may not all be true, but some of them are so extraordinary it is easier to imagine they were the haphazard spin-offs of life than of fancy.

Wind is responsible for a lot of naughtiness. A ghillie on Tulchan beat on the Spey was boating with a lady fiddling with her cast. The cast flew free and in the flip of the wind the fly got hooked in her lip. The fly-line that she had neglected to retrieve bellied out from the boat into fast water and as it started to pull on her lip she was obliged to jump into the river. It was perhaps one of the few times that the hooked victim had manoeuvred from the boat into the river and not vice versa. The painful episode was concluded when the cast was severed and she crawled ashore. Around the same time, also on the Spey, a man caught three fish on the same cast, two sea-trout on droppers and a salmon on the tail.

Big fish stories are often tedious, involving an empty net at the end. But even fishers who do not listen to other people's tell their own. A friend of mine on the Spey played a 40 pound fish for over two hours, taking turns with the man who had hooked it. In the interim the unattached fisherman hailed cars on the road for the use of a landing net, but of the three that stopped none had a net that was large enough. Eventually the big boy, which had hung about all this time in the outrun of the pool, rent the last vestiges of strength in the 18 pound nylon as its tormentors tried to haul it up the bank, and glided idly away. The big fish success story I like best is the late McDonald Hastings' catch on the Aberdeenshire Dee. Having waded too deep in fast water, when the fish struck the fisherman was pulled in by it, and moon-walking along the bottom up to his chin, was swept away. The weight of water in his waders held him upright and when his feet hooked round a big rock he got out to land the fish. The give-away phrase in his account is 'most of the time the rod-point was under the surface'.

The mis-hooking story the participants did not like so much was on a northern river and ended in a casualty ward. An old gentleman fishing in tweeds got a treble hook stuck in the seat of his plus fours. His shortsighted companion of the same vintage, bent down to find and release the fly but instead got it stuck in his nose. Somehow, by somebody, in this pose, they were conveyed to the doctor. The point about a fishing fly is that it is indiscriminate. Fish too, though, can be foolhardy and forgetful. Fishing on the North Esk the well known Spey angler, Mark Birkbeck, hooked a salmon with a worm, which broke him. Five casts later he caught it, this time with a fly, the first hook with the worm still on it in the fish's throat. The same sort of thing happened on the Helmsdale when my grandmother caught a fish with a size 10 Jeanie in the pool in which a fortnight before, a friend of hers had lost a fish with a size 6 Jeanie; his fly was still in its mouth.

Salmon are suckers (a fact not to be mentioned near fishermen); but muddled suckers. My grandmother once caught in the Helmsdale a salmon tagged as a kelt at 8 pounds in the Wye. Now, at the opposite end of Britain it had put on another 6 pounds. On the same theme, of fishing unaccountability, a salmon netted and tagged at Berriedale in Caithness was caught ten days later on the west coast of Ross-shire, re-tagged, and caught ten days later in the Berriedale nets again.

Fish behaviour, if you can spot it, is a useful guide. The

heaviest trout caught at Amhuinnsuidhe in Harris was hooked after the fisher had returned to the water a salmon parr. The parr floated off and was suddenly snapped in half from a mouth below. The second half floated for a minute more, then there was another swirl and that was gone. The fisherman put a small fly in the same general area and the sea-trout, believing its luck was really in, took that too.

Beginners tell us more about fishing than all the sententious experts. They blow our angling theories clean out of the water. In a particularly dour August on the Helmsdale the two male rod-hogs deigned to let their wives take the rods one hopeless afternoon. Both women were in advanced pregnancy, neither had fished before, and both caught a fish immediately. My father has fished for over 50 years and his heaviest fish was on the Helmsdale and it was also his first. His fishing friend Robin Duncanson rose a fish which would not come again, so he turned to walk back a yard or two and hooked a 27 pound salmon while the fly was trailing on the water's edge, the rod over his shoulder.

A six year old boy whom I know broke all records landing a 7 pound sea-trout on the Spey in 1991. When the fish struck he took fright, ran up the bank, fell over the labrador, still holding the rod, and discovered he had yanked the fresh fish onto dry land in 30 seconds. This was a mixed year for beginners on the Spey. Another fisherman hooked his first salmon and found after half an hour his fly line detach itself from the backing. Many people tried to find the fly line without success, but the next morning someone did. The fish was still on the end. The lucky fisherman attached the fly line to the backing again, replayed the fish, and then lost it for the second time. Maybe this was the longest time a first salmon has ever been on the end.

The old campaigners neither get, nor deserve, the sympathy we mete out to the beginners. One man who had just bought a timeshare on the Oykel fished all week without so much as a movement when on the Saturday he finally landed a fish. 'That blasted fish' he lamented to the ghillie 'along with my hotel and drink bill and travel has cost me £1,500'. 'Well,' commiserated the ghillie 'it's lucky you didn't catch another one then.' The Helmsdale had one doughty fisherman, a man well known for his catch records, who came annually for several weeks. 'I don't understand it' he complained to a local man one year, 'I haven't caught a fish all week.' 'Well, Sir' rightly observed his audience 'it's nice to see you are still breaking records.' Ghillies do have a way of putting things. Another Helmsdale fisher lady who should have known better

pulled the fly from the fish's mouth, before it could turn. 'Ach' moaned the ghillie 'you've stretched his neck!'

It is not for laughs we fish, but they sometimes come along with it. Some of the jokes must, on the occasion, remain private. I had two friends staying who were sharing a rod one summer partnered by a wily old man who had been in Africa. The old colonial's catch began to look good. After a few days it was clear he was having the fishing week of his life. No other two-rod beat on the river was catching as many as he was alone. Wherever he went he caught fish, both in front of my chums or behind them. As he grew in stature they became more forlorn. At lunch he lectured them on esoteric fly-tying techniques and fishing knots. They fished earlier and earlier and later and later to no avail. On the last day we devised a strategy for an evening cast on a pool we were sure the old boy didn't know about. As we arrived, out of the fading light we saw him struggling up the bank, several salmon dangling from his arms. It is not unfair to say that what rapture he got out of the week was paid for by their dismay. By the end everything, as happens on these occasions, had gone to pot, including their ability to cast. I think about it now with a smile, but had to keep a decently straight face at the time. Sporting achievement after all apes the larger patterns of life, success and reward coming in phases, but seldom in an unending flow.

In percentage terms, and logically, knowledge of the river counts enormously. I have heard from the mouths of many fishing tenants stories about a particularly salmon-wise proprietor on a neighbouring river in Sutherland. Once a tenant, at the utmost pitch of disappointment, after hours of fruitless casting, ventured to suggest to the proprietor that there really were no fish in the river at the time. They had run through, or fallen back, or not arrived. He was invited by the proprietor to the bank and to watch, while in artful fashion one neat lie was tried by this expert fisherman after the other. In a matter of an hour several fish adorned the bank.

I have been night-fishing for sea-trout on the Spey with six other rods when one was witnessed hooking 16 fish and between the rest of us we hooked only 2. There are certain conditions which separate the men who can use fishing rods from the boys who just carry them around.

Casting is part of the satisfaction of fishing, and you do not have to be holding the rod yourself. One of my most memorable fishing experiences was watching a local angler projecting a very long roll cast with great delicacy across shallow water above the main town bridge crossing the Ness. I can remember his almost mesmerically smooth style to this day. I have seen the master-fisher of the

Deveron, Andrew Tennant, collect a crowd just by fishing a pool which was viewable from a road bridge, with a line that arced in as telling a curve as the lion tamer's pinpoint whip-cracking in the ring. It feels good when one is casting well, as if one's own limbs had been elongated and empowered. When Andrew Tennant came to the Helmsdale the ghillie told me he knew he belonged to the small fraternity of master fishermen just by the way he held the rod walking down to the river.

The paradoxical thing is that using a fishing rod at this level of excellence the angler is not conscious of the rod, or casting; he is totally focused on the water. I noticed this in South Africa where the rainbow fishing is often in narrow streams almost hidden by tall grasses and with obstructive bushes and vegetation behind. The practised fishermen there never looked behind or to the side, they were bent on the water; and the line flying out behind somehow seldom got hooked up on the foliage, and if it did, at the very first touch of contact, they would flip it and again it would be working, looping through the air spaces and then falling unerringly on a tiny target area of water.

Scotland has the inestimable advantage of a long and well-larded tradition in fishing. It is the definitive fly fishing nation, which gave birth to the mighty green-heart cane rod. From the countries into which British colonists introduced game fish (South Africa, New Zealand) there are the countries in which British fishermen introduced the concept of sport angling for salmon (Norway, Iceland), and initiated fishing traditions. Such traditions involved almost entire life styles. Writers like Scrope, Buchan and Scott immortalised the character stereotypes who might be found on river and hill. Landseer and Andsell painted them. These people, the eagle-like ghillies, the doughty and sardonic stalkers, are here still, trained by their forebears in the art of presentation of sporting opportunity, consciously and unconsciously filling out the curiously compelling lineaments of tradition (maybe some poachers do this too). The compulsory evening dram sits on the table in front of the roaring fire in many a Highland hotel and shooting lodge. Bent old rods are on the wall, forgotten leathery-looking fish, smoke-coated stags heads. While the whisky is drunk the pattern of the day falls into place, its moments savoured and lodged in memory.

For these reasons the world's salmon fishermen and hunters want to visit Scotland and measure the legend against realities. The legal right to salmon and sea-trout fishing in Scotland being an absolute and heritable property right this may be done on exclusively private water as cannot be guaranteed in some other fishing nations. The same is true of stalking and most shooting rights, and Britain's long experience of game management, aided by the legal underpinning necessary for it, have served visiting sportsmen well.

It was in Britain that the old muskets were first replaced by the breech-loading double-barrelled shotguns, first seen in a London gunshop in 1853. This led to the tradition of winged game driven to shooting butts. The supreme sporting bird was the red grouse. The Highlands had heather moorland grouse habitat in plentiful supply and the traditions of grouse management, which perhaps started with grouse protection under Mary Queen of Scots, and which were established over the years, are practised with equal keenness today. Most grouse moors have fallen from their former peaks of productivity in terms of bags shot but, as some shooting writers have remarked, that might be no bad thing. (My father has in his game book an 800-plus grouse bag shot in a day at Gannochy in Angus, which corresponded exactly to the five year average bag in the season when the estate sold in the mid 1980s). The days when the skin of the loader's hands was singed from handling red-hot gun-barrels, as happened in the classic 1931 season at Glendye when over 17,000 grouse were shot, are unlikely to be experienced again in Scotland. But now a more varied pattern of bird and animal life dwells in the hills, which satisfies the moderated climate of opinion regarding a mixed use for land. Whether the grouse are flying in hundreds over the butts, or in tens, they still have a magnetic allure for shooting men unrivalled by any other bird.

Here is the shooting writer J. K. Stanford on the special quality of grouse:

'I think *mystique* is the right word, for the complete silence of their approach, the looming black forms which suddenly hurtle at you and over you, so uncannily magnified on a misty day, the immense distances from which they come and into which they disappear, are all in the highest degree mysterious, even after long acquaintanceship . . . they seem to come from the back of beyond, relentless in their onslaught, and even if they include the butts in their casual sweep, they surge on almost unscathed, a vast disordered, yet orderly procession of birds bound for some other place far behind you. They have played their part in the day's sport and have done with you for the rest of it.'

Stanford writes on the actual drive in a way that expresses his exhilaration:

'A line of drivers toils up a ridge and spreads out along the crest well over a mile away. You can just discern the flicker of a distant red flag and, long before you think it possible, the air high above you is full of dark birds, looking no bigger than thrushes but forging over the butts on powerful wings . . . Just as you reload, another wave of 20 or 30 birds, in line abreast, is sweeping on with relentless speed a few feet above the heather. You put up your gun as they come into shot, they rise a little, and next second a dark form spreadeagled in the air with legs down is hurling itself at your face. You have barely time to duck as it bounces to the ground five yards behind and the rest of the pack swishes three feet over your cap and are gone, unscathed.'

Or, Eric Parker:

' . . . it is a rather bigger lot of birds that break so quietly out of the sky and is over him and gone, with his two cartridges (as he knows) fired hopelessly behind the bird which (he realises as he pulls) he has picked too late out of the swirling, crossing forms. He jerks his cartridges out and feverishly loads again, and then . . . a single bird to his left front, on the sky line; he has hardly closed his gun, he throws it up without aiming, just looking at the bird, and — oh, incredible! — the dark form changes shape, blurs in mid-air, hurtles towards the heather 30 yards down the hill.'

Not only are driven grouse fast, they are unexpected. In Highland grouse butts on rolling ground, fields of fire vary, and every shooter faces a bird which is flying slightly differently. The wind varies too, so that successive visits to the same butts can still provide changing challenges. Birds can seem to hang in the air rounding a hill top, or they race towards you on a curve, travelling at 70 miles an hour. Stanford observes the speeds of individual birds may vary by 20 miles an hour, which is nearly 28 feet in a second. He describes one drive in tennis terminology as 'like playing a series of fast volleys at a net when you cannot see your opponent until the ball appears.'

Gossip about the season's grouse prospects quickens in July. By the end of June most guns who own or who have rented moors know how the nesting has fared. The challenge of grouse unites a catholic collection of shooters from many countries and many walks of life. They know as well as grouse proprietors that the birds' breeding success is legendarily uncertain; moors can be flush one year and bust the next. Part of the grouse's mystique is that even after a century of study it is not altogether clear why grouse behave as they do, why they pack when they do, how nature urges on them a survival tactic which involves suddenly departing their home moor, even their home county, sometimes to travel very long distances. The late Lord Biddulph, recognised for his tremendous reclamation of grouseland in the Lammermuirs, got on well with his American shooting tenants, who became used to the boom and bust cycles of grouse populations. Nonetheless he woke one night, during a woeful grouse season, with a tumult going on outside and strange lights flickering. On looking out he found his shooting tenants, some senior American businessmen, incinerating his effigy below his bedroom-window on the lawn. It says something for their recognition of his colossal sense of humour.

Shooting tenants can do many things to the proprietor or factor, but they seldom dumbfound them as the Egyptian tenants did who took a smart moor in Caithness. Here the grouse are shot in the old-fashioned way, two guns walking up behind a pointing dog. The shooting day was proceeding smoothly, and the fact that the guns were dressed in white robes instead of tweeds was not something a proprietor could look askance on, especially as the standard of marksmanship was extraordinarily good. Each gun had a bodyguard and the keepers were a little surprised to see one of this ilk, also swathed in white, stalking forward quietly over the hill in a different direction. The man lunged into the heather, pounced, and stood up clutching a startled grouse which, with a flash of his dagger, he beheaded. Evidently the follower of Mahomet cannot eat a grouse killed by lead; it must be cut by steel facing Mecca. This unfortunate bird was for the master's table. History does not relate the keeper's comment, but one suspects even the Highlander's off-the-cuff remark might have been wanting in the circumstances.

On occasion no comments can be worse than to-the-point ones. My grouse shooting career started ominously. My grandmother's grouse moor, as it was then, had a smart entourage including one or two noted shots from Norfolk. I was in my early teens and allowed to go into the occasional point, wide of the guns, far out on the wings. This normally gave me time to see the bird get going and if it came my way I could have a swing at it. This time the dog started following a running grouse which had gone uphill to where I stood, a small figure on the skyline. Without consciously having done so I had slipped off the safety catch and, in the expectation of a shot at any moment, was fingering the trigger. An explosion went off followed by flying earth and vegetation. I looked down at a smoking crater which had appeared in front of my left foot. The keeper was apparently unconcerned, and when I went to see him later he observed that I would never do such a thing again; but the guns muttered a bit and one glanced at me with what I suppose was apprehension. My physical distance from the other guns was tactfully extended a bit.

Trigger-happy youths aside, shooting over dogs is a

wonderfully rhythmic and civilised way of combining sport and healthy exercise with the appreciation of working dogs and the views and changing scenery. Although most shots are taken at birds flying away from the guns there is still considerable variety in the shooting challenge, and a high wind can validate the old quip that on some days grouse fly quicker than lead. Shooting over dogs or in the line of guns is a more social sporting occasion, and guns and keepers intermingle in a way that happens less naturally in the butt. Two good friends shooting together over dogs can carve out some very happy memories.

Two good friends had just enjoyed such a day on the Caithness moor, Langwell. Its proprietor the Duke of Portland was happily disputing with his fellow nobleman from Ireland, Enniskillen, whether grouse were bigger in Caithness or in Ireland. To settle the matter the Duke despatched his keeper to sally forth and shoot the biggest cock grouse he could find on Langwell, while Enniskillen telegraphed to have a similar specimen sent over from his moor. His Grace decided finally to settle the matter by instructing his keeper clandestinely to fill his bird's crop with lead shot. At the weigh-in the Scottish grouse looked the easy victor, until its head tipped out of the scales and shot fell out rattling on the table. 'The game is up' conceded the Duke.

Grouse are generous birds in what they offer man. Scotland has become a destination for falconers from all over. Moor owners today can ask substantial rents from falconers who only use a small part of the ground for a few hours in the afternoon, and count a bag of one brace as a success. The older generation of keepers were at first sceptical about falconry and the artificial introduction into grouse territories of the bird their forebears had so strenuously tried to keep off it. These fears have been allayed over time as it has been shown that peregrines flying overhead fix grouse most effectively on home-beats, and that of the very few birds killed often the falcon singles out weaker individuals which would anyway be premature casualties of the season. The aim of falconry is to find the closest match between the flying skills of predator and prey, and in many places in the Highlands falconry now offers a spectacular event which adds as much to the season as the rent does to the landlord's purse.

Substantially the Highlands offers the same as it did in shooting terms to the early Victorians. The decline in variety of game shooting which pushed English sportsmen northwards in the early 19th century has continued. The great game shooting opportunities in the Highlands remain much the same, and all of it is natural shooting, of wild birds. Here only can capercailzie be shot, considered

by some to be the trickiest shooting target of all, huge to stop yet deceptively trim in the air, rocketing past when they had seemed hardly to be moving in front, appearing suddenly at unexpected angles and incalculable speeds.

The snipe shooting, driven or walked up, in the islands, is unsurpassed. Tiree and South Uist are renowned for flat bogs full of this difficult quarry. Snipe shooting means cartridge-bags emptying faster than game-bags fill up; the bird quivers rather than flies and also twists from side to side. One of the owners of South Uist Estate told me how it brought on young shooters to let them loose there, where only instinctive split-second shooting can bring home the supper. The Western Isles also intercept migrating woodcock in boggling numbers. In the largely unwooded islands the woodcock tend to concentrate on the few oases of trees and are therefore relatively easy to find. The Scottish islands in general offer unique richness of variety to shooting people. Geography and climate have magnified the islanders' natural disinclination to effect major land-use changes, and bequeath to the adventurous shooter wonderful possibilities for completely natural sport. The wild-fowling is legendary, and shooting literature has many stories of intrepid wild-fowlers landing on isles in the west that are little more than semi-submerged platforms, and waiting patiently for passing duck as the tide off the Atlantic rises.

At the other end of the altitude spectrum is the sport to be had on the high tops. Ptarmigan adopt a whiter plumage in winter to blend into the snow-striped scree which is the minimalist habitat from which they eke a living. Shooting them expends all spare energy and taps the hidden reserves. Generally they stick to the mountain top they live on, and fly round the ridges on which the shooters are toiling. Hitting one is a challenging thing, usually against a backdrop of mountain-ranges and glens marching to the horizon. If this seems exhausting, consider the alternative method employed in Scandinavia: skiing after them armed with a small bore rifle.

Sometimes Highland sport can be physically complicated as well as tiring. Take rock pigeon shooting off the north of Scotland. A small boat ferries the shooters to the foot of a cliff. There in the choppy slap of waves hitting stone the boat pitches sickeningly while the shooters try to zero in on rock pigeons whizzing out of the caves which are their homes. The combination of talents needed to perfect this art are notoriously elusive, and the whole gambit can be made more testing, if required, by rougher weather.

A famous sport of the past was driven hare shooting. Numbers of both brown and mountain hares are declining, but hare shoots still exist in places. Sometimes a remnant of moorland gradually enclosed by forestry, and therefore redundant for grouse shooting, produces good hare populations, especially off the rich farmlands of Aberdeenshire. Hares can speed towards the butts in the same numbers as grouse, and provide exciting sport.

When the early Victorians first surged north in search of wild game in wild country they came to a land in which land-use changes had happened slowly. The landscape they saw has changed remarkably little since. Sporting use has been the friend of preserved landscapes and wildlife diversity. The only major change has been since the last war, with the plantation of big tracts with forestry. This development has produced sporting uses of its own with the resurgence in the Highlands of large numbers of roe deer. In places the roe have even colonised habitats on open moorland, never returning to tree-cover even at night. Woodland stalking in Britain lacks the tradition and long-term experience enjoyed by the continentals, but gradually the scene is changing and the sporting values of this extremely testing craft are becoming understood. The last ten years have been a period of retrenchment for foresters as sporting-use facilities have been cut into woodlands in the form of rides and glades. There are parts of the Highlands where a woodland stalker might encounter roe, red or sika deer, each with different habitats and different deer-trots criss-crossing each other through the trees. With the long deer shooting season of these species collectively, the possibilities for fun are prodigious. Woodland stalking can result in very close encounters.

One such happened to me in 1991. In the corner of a forestry block which is too steep for trees I spied the antlers of a big stag at dusk. Challenged by a young royal on the hilltop beyond the fence-line the stag was distracted from noticing my uphill approach at close quarters, which otherwise would have been detected. As I reached the top of the knoll he had been lying on I saw him further down the deer-fence, a very large black stag in the twilight, emerging from the trees for the first time as the roaring of the open-hill stags announced the onset of the rut. The stag turned to face the fence, put his heavily-antlered head into the horizontal wires, and with one quick heave of his bushy neck jerked the adjacent deer-posts from their holes into the air. Bending and twisting the wires he stepped through the gap he had created, stretched his body, and stood against the darkening horizon emitting a low epiglottal roar. He then trotted off in search of action. Such sights stay in the mind as long as anything in stalking.

The photographer who can put flesh on the bones of spectacle is Glyn Satterley. His photographs describe the estate system from the inside outwards. He has a canny knack of getting the feeling behind the dramatic scene. The Highlands' stupendous physical beauty has not been allowed to call the tune, although it provides a memorable setting for what happens. Rather, he manages to show what it is like, experientially, to live and work in the hills.

When he first came up to the Highlands in the late 1970s the buoyant character from Kent was struck by the individuals he encountered. They made an indelible impression on him for their developed and durable characters, wry sense of humour, and ability to unfold a view of life that had little in common with city folk. It is a view of life tempered by living alongside wild country and untrammelled nature. It fascinated him, and a challenge materialised — to get it on film and to show it from the inside.

Since then he has walked many miles shouldering his cameras. He has covered huge tracts of the Highlands in the company of its indigenous people. He has a way of blending into the background at the vital moment, and many of the more intimate studies would never have been possible unless he had established relationships of companionship and trust with the individuals that he photographed. He approached the sporting scene without preconceptions and took people as he found them.

The photographs themselves stir different responses in people. By any standards they are unusual, some would say quirkish. They are taken by someone who is himself neither a shooting man nor a fisherman: when he puts down the camera he reaches for his golf clubs. The photographs are those of an outsider looking in to a way of life which has absorbing interest for him. The visual images and their juxtapositions can have an ambiguous quality, usually a result of pinpointing curious activities carved out against a dramatic, often theatrical, backdrop. They are nearly always striking, often witty. None of these are set-up shots. They were all taken in the course of routine activities. Those selected here are a fraction of the total he has assembled over 12 years, a collection which now forms part of Scotland's sporting history.

Like most photographs these depend, initially, on being in the right place at the right time. Glyn Satterley has spent a lot of time in a lot of different places to get them. If they serve as a tribute to transitory passages in many people's working lives they also celebrate a venerable institution. The Highland sporting estate has had many eloquent witnesses and chroniclers who have testified in print. Here is one with an eloquent eye.

The Highland Game

COULIN LANDSCAPE, TORRIDON, WESTER ROSS.
The Coulin countryside evokes classic Highland grandeur, accentuated by some Scots Pines which have been wonderfully misshapen by over 300 years of Torridonian weather. The estate nurtures one of the remaining pockets of the ancient Caledonian Forest, which once covered most of Northern Scotland.

LOCHDHU LODGE, ALTNABREAC, CAITHNESS.
The Victorian estate owners often built their lodges in
the most remote and awe-inspiring locations. This
Caithness lodge is no exception. It gradually appears,
like a mirage on the horizon, when you have driven mile
upon mile through peat bog and heather. Sadly, from
both an environmental and visual point of view, this
landscape is about to change drastically. The whole area
has been planted, boundary to boundary, with conifers;
slowly the mirage will disappear.

KEEPERS' COMMUTING VEHICLE, BORROBOL, SUTHERLAND.
The Argocat amphibious vehicle has become as indispensable to the Highland keeper as the four-wheeled motorcycle has to the hill shepherd. The modern version of the hill-pony, it has made life a lot easier, particularly on boggy and hilly countryside.

SPRINGTIME HEATHER BURNING, AUCHENTOUL, SUTHERLAND.
This annual activity conjures up great nostalgia for anyone who has taken part. Lunch amidst a smouldering landscape, eating sandwiches with blackened hands. Clothes that will reek for days to come. Controlled strip burning is done on grouse moors to regenerate plant growth and create different heights of heather to provide shelter and food. Elsewhere, general burnings are done for the benefit of sheep and deer. As you can imagine, in windy conditions, controlling this spread of fire becomes difficult. Local folklore tells of several occasions when the burning got out of hand. Recently, a particular fire started in central Sutherland, burnt a path stretching 40 miles, stopping only when it hit the North coast.

CONSTRUCTING A DEER FEEDER, SUISGILL, SUTHERLAND.
Today, more and more estates feed their wintering red deer herd in order to help them survive the harsh weather, and keep them in better condition. It also encourages the deer to stay on estate ground. Here keeper Donny McKay is gauging the height of his feeder carefully, so that none of the hay goes to the estate sheep.

FEEDING STAGS, KERNSARY, WESTER ROSS.

This feeding station at Kernsary, is one of five that Dougie Russell tends each afternoon throughout the winter and spring. It was remarkable to see the rapport that Dougie has developed with these deer as one wrong move from me and they would be off over the horizon — their wild instinct intact. It was also impressive that he would arrive at a feeding station and if it was deserted, he would spend up to half an hour periodically bawling out 'Come on' to the deserted landscape. Sure enough they would eventually appear on the skyline, like red Indians spying down on the cavalry, and then come in to the feed. Dougie would explain where they had probably been that day due to weather or hill walker disturbance, and he would also note with concern any absentees. He seemed to know them all. This Letterewe policy of feeding with extra nutrients, helps sustain the deer through the winter, encourages new antler growth and puts the hinds in good breeding condition.

CULLING HINDS, KINTAIL, KYLE, ROSS-SHIRE.
It is not surprising that few people are prepared to pay to shoot the female red deer, since this is done during the severest months of the winter Most hinds are culled by estate keepers, as one of their routine jobs, and usually they tackle it single-handed.

OPPOSITE
SPRINGTIME FOX CULLING — CHECKING A DEN.
Springtime foxing activities are legend throughout the Highlands. Keepers and shepherds regard the fox as a threat to both grouse and lambs, and come springtime, they pursue it vigorously, night and day. Most keepers are familiar with every inch of their ground, and know all suitable den sites. These are regularly watched for signs of life, and if suspected of harbouring a new litter of cubs, terriers are sent in.

SPRINGTIME FOX CULLING — MIDNIGHT CHECK TO SEE DEN IS STILL BLOCKED OFF.

Within a fortnight of the cubs being born the vixen leaves them in the den, keeping an eye on them from a safe distance. She will only return to feed them, and when danger threatens. After a daytime onslaught by the terriers, even though it is suspected the vixen is away, the den will be blocked off. The keeper then revisits it at night, and by means of a tape-recorder, the fox will be lured towards a spotlight and the rifle.

SPRINGTIME FOX CULLING — VIXEN SHOT BY AID OF SPOTLIGHT AND TAPE.

The keeper is pleased with himself, not merely because he has killed this vixen, but because it is the culmination of a couple of weeks work and planning, and the end of at least one threat to the grouse he is employed to protect.

This particular culling took place miles from anywhere in the middle of the Sutherland Flow Country. It was a bizarre experience to be out there at midnight. As the taped cries echoed eerily in the dark, snow began to fall, and through a flurry the eyes of the fox shone in the spotlight, until the rifle fired.

STALKER, JOHN ROSS, WITH HIS SPRING LAMBS, KYLESTROME ESTATE, SUTHERLAND.
Most keepers seem to have an inborn dislike of sheep, which is often aggravated when they are called upon to help out during lambing and clipping. There are exceptions of course, John Ross being one. He has happily taken on the role of shepherd, as well as stalker, throughout the year. To see his dogs efficiently gather and pen ewes with new born lambs, you would think it was his only job.

AUGUST LAMB SALES, LAIRG, SUTHERLAND.
For a lot of northern estates the Lairg lamb sales in early August provide their only real agricultural harvest. Lairg, virtually a ghost town, outwith the odd tourist influx, benefits as well. The town is engulfed by a huge fleet of livestock floats, 30,000 plus North Country Cheviot lambs, buyers from all over Britain, estate owners, shepherds, crofters, wives, children, tourists and collies of all descriptions. The best atmosphere is to be sampled either in the turmoil of the sale rings, or in the vicinity of the stockmen's refreshment hut.

ANGUS ROSS, WITH DEAD MOLES, ACHENTOUL, SUTHERLAND.
Since the demise of many estate gardens, the aesthetic blight of molehills is something few keepers are expected to deal with these days. The lodge lawn at Achentoul, however, still survives intact thanks to Angus's enthusiastic moleing expertise.

FEMALE SALMON TRANSPORT, RIVER HELMSDALE, SUTHERLAND.
In the autumn, netted salmon hens are ceremoniously transported from the river in a coffin-like container to oxygenated tanks. They are then taken to the hatchery, stripped of their eggs, and returned to the river. The eggs are carefully nurtured until they grow into smolts, and are returned to the Helmsdale as small fish.

OPPOSITE
DONNY TAKES A BREAK BY THE AGA, SUISGILL, SUTHERLAND.
The Aga, or Rayburn, takes pride of place in most keepers' kitchens. Not as the pristine, co-ordinated mod-con we see in country magazines, but as the harbourer of all that the keeper is likely to wear and use in a day's work. It warms his boots, backside, rifle, binoculars, hat, mitts, and his dogs when they can get near it. His wife will cook food in it and there's always a kettle on it anticipating a cup of tea. This particular one has even dried out the odd lens, not to mention a very grateful photographer on a number of occasions.

KEEPERS' NEW YEAR HARE DRIVE, BLAIR ATHOLL, PERTHSHIRE, 1985.
One of the perks for the Blair Atholl keepers was, until recently, the annual hare shoot, a day given over to them by the Duke of Atholl. Sandy Reid, the head keeper, invited the 'guests', mainly keepers and friends from neighbouring estates, and a sweepstake was organised on the number of hares shot. The past couple of years have however seen the Estate letting out more and more of its hare shooting, at the expense of the keepers' day out.

HAVING A SUIT FITTED, CAMPBELLS OF BEAULY, ROSS-SHIRE.

Keepers were traditionally given a new tweed suit each season, paid for by the estate. It usually arrived in time for the twelfth of August grouse, or to herald a new stalking season, in the smartest manner. Twelve months on and they don't look quite so smart, having been through heather, burns, peat bog, and the washing machine a good many times. Keepers swear they are as weather tight and considerably warmer than the much heralded waxed jacket. However, proving to be practically indestructible in this cost cutting era has had its drawbacks and the tweed suit has now become bi-annual. There used to be numerous shops in the Highlands making these suits but today the likes of Campbells is a rarity.

PAST AND PRESENT STAFF OF REAY FOREST ESTATE, SEPTEMBER 1985. LOCHMORE LODGE, ACHFARRY.

Photographs like this were taken on most estates annually. It shows Anne, Duchess of Westminster, centre, surrounded by her staff and their children. The staff represented includes stalkers, river and hill ghillies, pony men, house maids, the factor, handyman, chauffeur, gardener, cook, and personal maid. Today this kind of gathering is unique and most estates have reduced staff to a minimum. Owners entertain guests far less and let the lodge, as well as the sport, for a good part of the season. Reay Forest Estate, and in particular Lochmore Lodge was an exception. The Duchess ran the lodge on traditional lines, with plenty of staff — some permanent at Lochmore, others coming up from Chester for the season.

The lodge interior was immaculate, extremely comfortable, and guests were treated like royalty. I was kindly invited into this unfamiliar world by the Duchess, after having photographed one of her guests out stalking. The lifestyle was a new experience for me and as one of very few Highland households still operating that way I felt it needed recording . The Duchess agreed wholeheartedly and gave me the freedom of the house. Her guests and staff without exception, all co-operated as I covered both the 'upstairs' and 'downstairs' life of the lodge. They proved to be an important set of photographs because the Duchess left Lochmore in 1986 and moved to a smaller house on the estate. She continues to live in the same style, but Lochmore was let the following year.

WYVIS LODGE, ROSS-SHIRE.
Most lodges, whatever their location, prove to be a disappointment when you first lay eyes on them. I have driven miles, down the worst 'roads' imaginable, in anticipation of finding the ultimate lodge. Discoveries on Ordnance Survey maps would set me off optimistically, as would comments such as . . . 'it's the most magnificently isolated building on the West'. More often than not I'd get there to find it hidden by a mature belt of trees, demolished, or even sunk beneath some raised Hydro scheme loch. Wyvis is one of the few lodges not to disappoint, lying as it does in stately isolation at the head of Loch Glass, for all to see.

CUTTING THE VERGES, ARDVERIKIE LODGE.
This monster of a building was almost chosen by Queen
Victoria, in preference to Balmoral. Before visiting there
I had only glimpsed it across Loch Laggan like other
motorists on the Spean Bridge to Dalwhinnie road.
Little did I imagine the scale of what was lurking over
there.

'OPENING-UP' LOCH STACK LODGE, REAY FOREST ESTATE.
Traditionally lodges were closed down at the end of the season, usually at the end of October after the stalking had finished. They were re-opened again in April or May as the fishing and weather improved. I felt as if time had stopped, as I wandered through these rooms, surrounded by the still shrouded shapes.

THESE NEXT FIVE PHOTOGRAPHS WERE TAKEN ON VISITS TO LOCHMORE LODGE AND SHOW VARIOUS STAFF AT WORK.

JESSIE DUSTING THE DUCHESS'S STUDY, LOCHMORE LODGE, 1985.

THE 'UPSTAIRS' BREAKFAST TRAY, LOCHMORE LODGE, 1985.

MRS ARMSTRONG LAYING OUT BREAKFAST, LOCHMORE LODGE, 1985.

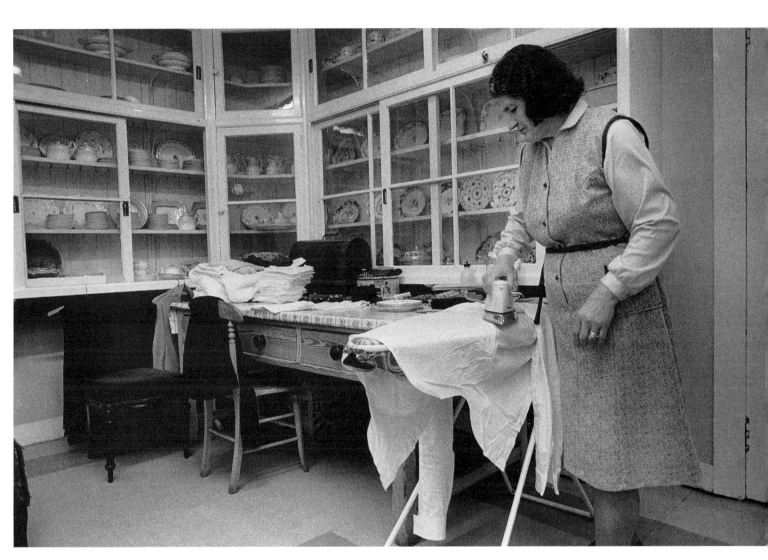

JESSIE IRONING GUESTS' LAUNDRY, LOCHMORE LODGE, 1985.

PREPARING THE LUNCH PACKS, LOCHMORE LODGE, 1985.

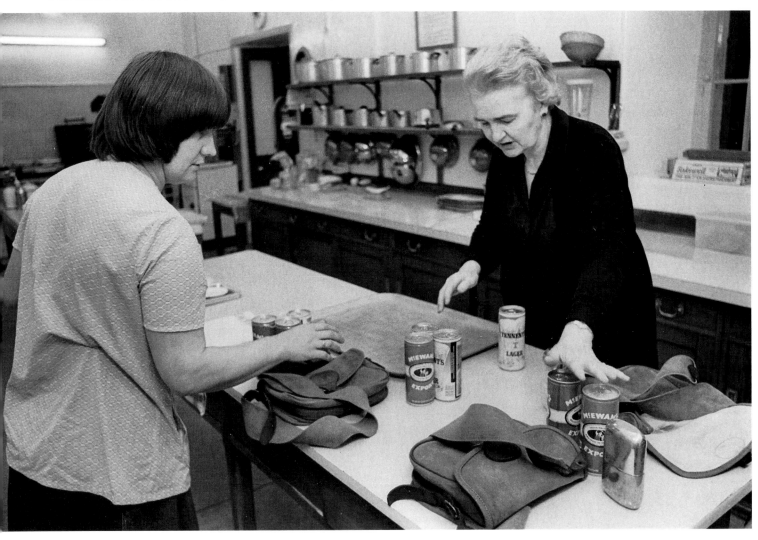

PHEASANT SHOOT GATHERING, BLAIR CASTLE, PERTHSHIRE.
It is customary for the keepers, loaders, beaters and dog handlers to gather in front of Blair Castle awaiting the morning's instructions. The 'guns' and guests assemble on the other side of the castle in the Duke's courtyard.

Each morning throughout the grouse season, the guests
at Invercauld are met by a formidable sight. Twelve
keepers all dressed in Farquharson tweed, looking like a
small army, waiting to escort them to the hill.

PREPARING TO GO LOCH FISHING, AMHUINNSUIDHE CASTLE, ISLE OF HARRIS.
Many first time visitors to Scotland are unprepared for the ferocity of the midge. Even Harris's beautiful scenery can't deter them.

Leaping Salmon, River Mouth, Loch Leosavay, Amhuinnsuidhe Castle.
During dry summer spells there is not enough water running in some rivers to attract home-coming salmon and sea trout back into the system. Consequently they hang around the mouth of the river, impatiently awaiting rain.

THE MORNING CONVOY LEAVES INVERCAULD FOR THE GROUSE MOORS.

THE PRELIMINARY SPY, FOREST OF HARRIS, ISLE OF HARRIS.

54

THE LOADERS MAKING THEIR WAY TO THE BUTTS, INVERCAULD.

MORNING ASSEMBLY OF FISHERMEN AND GHILLIES, THE GRIMERSTA RIVER SYSTEM, ISLE OF LEWIS.
The assembled party looked ready to take on the world, out in this empty backwater of Lewis. They slipped off quietly, motoring down the loch, and disappeared into the landscape. Six hours later they re-appeared in similar military style.

GOING TO THE HILL, INVERCAULD.
This eccentric looking procession, high on a remote Grampian hillside, is led into action by the kilted Laird of Invercauld, Capt. Farquharson, and his keepers. From the castle, they are whisked here, at least 5 miles from the nearest road, by a fleet of Land Rovers, and released into the landscape. It all reminded me of a lavish film production.

CAUTIOUSLY ADVANCING THROUGH THE PEAT HAGS, STALKING, GLENGINGIE, INVERNESS-SHIRE.
The actual stalk, after a suitable stag has been spied, can take hours. The wind can change, mist rolls in, and things like snow, or the discovery of a raging burn between the rifle and the beast can slow down the process still further. The autumn Highland landscape and weather together can prove a lethal combination, but in my experience, no party has ever turned back . . . 'just because of the weather . . . '

These creeping, crawling rituals are fascinating to watch, acted out amongst the wildest of backdrops.

OPPOSITE
SPYING FROM A BOAT, ISLE OF JURA.
Use of a boat, when stalking on islands, such as Jura, enables the party to cover ground that would be inaccessible from the land. I found the idea of a floating observatory amusing initially, but after a couple of hours of bobbing around like a cork, I felt sick. I could feel no sympathy for the stag they eventually brought on board, I just wanted to get ashore.

DRAWING PEGS FOR BUTT POSITIONS, INVERCAULD.
Each morning the guns 'draw' for their butt positions for the first drive of the day. At subsequent drives they move two butts on. This is the usual system on most British driven moors, but as many of Invercauld's paying guests are from overseas there are some delightful moments of confusion.

ERECTING THE CANES, INVERCAULD.
To the casual observer these temporary additions to the grouse butt may appear a bit fussy. They do have a function nevertheless: to stop the over-enthusiastic gun from shooting directly 'down the line' towards his neighbour. They don't however give much reassurance when you are trying to photograph butt action, a little way away.

FALCONERS GOING TO THE MOOR, CAITHNESS.

Many northern grouse moors are used extensively by falconers. Caithness flow country, with its vast flat landscape is ideal, particularly for viewing. The theatrical-like procession belies the seriousness of the sport though. There is intense concentration involved in getting the chosen hawk ready to fly. Then the pointer is released and immediately gets 'on point'. With its hood removed the bird takes off, and climbs higher and higher above the motionless dog and begins to circle. On command, the dog moves in and a grouse emerges, rocketing away just above the heather. The hawk needs no command, but makes for the grouse, gaining fast. They are about to collide, when instinctively the grouse flips to one side, and the hawk carries on, levelling out and flies out of sight. The master falconer, tracking device in hand, takes off in pursuit. I have seen this happen several times and for all its seriousness, never yet seen a grouse killed.

SPYING, COULIN ESTATE, ROSS-SHIRE.
The early stages of a stalk are constantly interrupted by spying sessions. The uninitiated eye, even with the aid of binoculars, will glean very little from the subtle autumn landscape. The instinctive eye of the stalker, however, not only spots any deer around, at immense distances, but at a glance can assess their condition, age and 'shootability'. Obsessed with spying, and hidden behind traditional check camouflage, they forget they too are being observed.

A WALK THROUGH THE FOREST OF HARRIS, STALKING, ISLE OF HARRIS.

I was always puzzled to see marked on O/S maps various forests throughout Highland upland regions, and barely a tree in sight when you were there. Of course these have been explained as deer forests, which were created in the last century, as the accepted stalking ground of each estate. I still wonder at vast areas of boulder strewn mountainside being described as a forest.

LOCH VOSHMID, NORTH HARRIS ESTATE, ISLE OF HARRIS.
This loch, set in such a superb location, is renowned for
its salmon and sea trout fishing. On this occasion I
suspect the conditions suited me far more than the
fishermen who by late afternoon had only caught one
small trout.

OPPOSITE
GHILLIE AND FISHERMAN, LOCH STACK, N.W. SUTHERLAND.

SPYING FROM THE TOP OF THE LODGE PATH, REAY FOREST, SUTHERLAND.

Anne, Duchess of Westminster, is an active and very enthusiastic stalker, and has been so most of her life. The only concession she allows herself in recent years is to ride one of the ponies up onto higher ground where stalking is likely to commence.

WORKING TOGETHER, PHEASANT SHOOT, BLAIR CASTLE,
PERTHSHIRE.
Col. Campbell-Preston and Blotto worked together, as if
they both knew what the other was thinking — save the
odd indiscretion by Blotto who occasionally tried to
chase a bird before it had been shot.

DOGGING FOR GROUSE, LANGWELL ESTATE, CAITHNESS.
Most people think the moorlands of Caithness are unrelentingly flat. I'm sure many of the Langwell guests, when
brought out grouse shooting, cannot believe their eyes when they see Morven's volcanic mass looming on the horizon.

Dogging For Grouse, Langwell Estate, Caithness.

THE SHOOTING PARTY SHELTERING FROM A SHOWER,
LANGWELL ESTATE.
Lunchtime on a grouse moor. The party which has
worked, walked, and talked together all morning,
separates into two groups — the 'guns' and their guests,
keepers and dog handlers — to eat their sandwiches a
discreet distance apart. On this occasion a sudden
downpour ended lunch prematurely.

THE LAIRD'S BUTT, INVERCAULD ESTATE, ABERDEENSHIRE.
As Laird of Invercauld, one would think that Capt. Farquharson would at least have a loader in his butt like all his paying guests. He doesn't go along with that idea and spends much of the day loading for himself. Rarely is he able to spend much of the day on his own however as the American guests see it as a great honour to be able to accompany the Laird in his butt for the duration of a drive. This time he was being accompanied by Moira Lister, a family friend.

THE LOADER AND THE HUNGARIAN COUNT, INVERCAULD
GROUSE BUTTS.

THE BEATERS APPEARING ON THE SKYLINE, GLENFIDDICH ESTATE, ABERDEENSHIRE.
This picture looks like the other side are ready to 'throw in the towel'. I wouldn't blame them if they were, as beaters walk up to three miles each drive, usually five drives a day. By the time the flags are this visible a loud horn or whistle will have sounded signalling that the guns must only shoot behind.

OPPOSITE
HOW TO SUPPRESS AN OVER ENTHUSIASTIC RETRIEVER, INVERCAULD GROUSE MOOR.

THE DUKE DISPENSES ELEVEN O'CLOCK REFRESHMENTS, PHEASANT SHOOT, BLAIR CASTLE, PERTHSHIRE.

GETTING WITHIN RANGE, INVERARAY ESTATE, ARGYLL.
The final moments of the crawl-in are tense, even for the observer.

RANDOLPH'S LEAP, RIVER FINDHORN, MORAYSHIRE.
Whatever difficulties the Findhorn poses fishermen, it is
very impressive how it has dramatically carved its way
down through the rocky landscape at Relugas.

THE WAY THEY DO THINGS ON THE SPEY, TULCHAN BEAT.

MEGAN BOYD, SALMON FLY TIER, BRORA, SUTHERLAND.

Megan Boyd worked from a tiny garden shed, overlooking a beautiful stretch of sandy coastline just north of Brora, in East Sutherland. From here, she created salmon flies without equal; masterpieces of the fishing world. Her speciality was, in her own words . . . 'All the old fancy patterns like Jock Scott, Silver Doctor, Black Doctor and Hairy Mary. Now they just stick together a bunch of hair, but I used to tie the flies with all the best of stuff.' Evidence of this was borne out in her cosy Aladdin's cave of a workshop, which was hung with feathers of every description, and had all manner of threads and materials poking from drawers and littering surfaces. Her flies were mainly supplied to devotees of the Northern rivers such as the Helmsdale, Brora, Thurso, and Naver. Megan tied flies all her working life, beginning as a schoolgirl at the age of 14. Ironically she prided herself with always trying to make the best fly possible for the job, but hated the idea that it would enable somebody to kill with it. Sadly in recent years she has been forced to give up because of diminished sight, but continues to be her inspirational and optimistic self.

THE CASTER, RIVER FINDHORN, THE LOGIE BEAT, RELUGAS, MORAYSHIRE.

NEARLY IN THE NET, TULCHAN BEAT, RIVER SPEY.
To photograph fishing successfully requires about as much patience and luck as the fisherman himself. You are always aware of the need to keep a low profile, in case you are blamed for the fish not taking. It is therefore very satisfying to be there when a fish is actually landed, dispelling the Jonah tag. In actual fact this one got away, and I took it as my cue to slip away quietly.

Sandy 'BadnaBay', Fishing Ghillie, River Laxford.
Sandy is one of those ghillies with that rare quality of
character, which makes guests request his company
year after year. He's just helped the Duchess land this
fish in The Duke's Pool.

ARDVORLICH BUTTS, LOCHEARNHEAD, PERTHSHIRE.
These butts, high up on the south side of Loch Earn, offer a far more spectacular perspective than normally found on Grampian or Inverness-shire grouse moors. The advantages of seeing the birds coming, possibly half a mile away, were however balanced out by the gale force wind speeds, which took them safely past these guns at about 120 miles per hour. Fortunately for me the butts also acted as a very efficient wind break, in addition to hiding the guns from the approaching birds.

GROUSE 'BLOODING', SUTHERLAND ESTATE
This ritual is akin to that practised in fox hunting, when a person riding with the hunt for the first time is daubed on the face with blood from the dead fox. On Highland estates it is more commonly carried out during stalking than it is on a grouse moor.

LUNCHTIME GATHERING, GROUSE SHOOT, ARDVORLICH,
LOCHEARNHEAD, PERTHSHIRE.
At Ardvorlich they still use ponies to collect the bags of
grouse, a sight rarely seen today. To the delight of most
of the paying guests the horses join the lunchtime
gathering, and are the centre of attention. Even they
had trouble polishing off the vast packed lunches the
guests had brought with them from Gleneagles.

CRAWLING-IN, STALKING, SUISGILL ESTATE, SUTHERLAND.
As well as stamina and the ability to ignore whatever the elements throw at him, the stalker needs the stealth of a cat to remain hidden. In terrain such as the flattish, rolling landscape of east Sutherland, stalkers will be called upon to crawl long distances in order to stay out of sight. It took me back to my childhood as they disappeared ahead of me over the brow.

ABOUT TO FIRE, ROE DEER STALK, REVAK WOODS, NETHY BRIDGE.

With the post-war expansion in forestry throughout the Highlands, particularly conifer plantations, the roe deer population has exploded. Culling is necessary and, as with red deer stags, people will pay to do it. The method of stalking a roe, however, varies dramatically from that of the red deer. The stalker is usually unaccompanied, as absolute silence and stealth are necessary, and he is usually within the vicinity of trees, rather than on the hill. There are two acceptable methods — either sitting, in wait, on a 'high' seat, or actually stalking through and around a plantation. Carried out either at dawn or dusk, creeping noiselessly through a dense plantation, requires a steady nerve even to watch.

MRS PANCHAUD'S JULY STAG, NORTH HARRIS ESTATE, ISLE OF HARRIS.

Traditionally stalking is carried out in the autumn, with its blustery, unpredictable weather, and the landscape dying back. Officially though, the season starts in July. This stag was killed on a beautiful Hebridean summer's day, high on the North Harris hills. The views were stunning; looking north or south you could see virtually the whole of the outer islands. With hardly a breath of wind around we were soon peeling layers of clothing off rather than adding them as is the norm while stalking. Then shortly after a relaxing picnic lunch Mrs Panchaud, the estate owner, competently despatched her stag, which was gralloched, and carried off the hill. She and her guest then decided to enjoy the weather, and set off to try and catch a salmon. It made me understand why they prefer to stalk in the autumn.

GRALLOCHING A STAG, REAY FOREST ESTATE, SUTHERLAND.
Gralloching (disembowelling), although not a pretty sight, is a very necessary part of the process to get the carcase to the game dealer in the best of condition. Once removed the gralloch is not wasted as it is left on the hill to be consumed by local residents such as eagles and ravens.

LOSING THE HEAD, NORTH HARRIS ESTATE, ISLE OF
HARRIS.
Normally the head of a stag is taken back to the larder
attached to the carcase. This one was still in velvet,
since it was shot early in the summer so it was left out
for carrion eaters.

STALKING LUNCHBREAK, BEN ARMINE, SUTHERLAND.
A stalking lunch is far less formal than that on the
grouse moor or on the river. Out on the hill it is grabbed
whenever proceedings, or weather allow.

RETRIEVING A FALCON, GARTYMORE, SUTHERLAND.
This is a piece of equipment most falconers I have met are familiar with. My most vivid recollections of any days spent with falconers are of seeing a figure charging across the heathery landscape with one of these aerials thrust skywards, trying to get a fix on the absconded bird.

DAVID WOODLEY, FALCONER, GARTYMORE, SUTHERLAND.

SALMON NETTING, THE SHORELINE, BERRIEDALE, CAITHNESS.
Since I took this picture in 1980, the netting of salmon at rivermouths and in rivers, has become very contentious. The number of salmon returning to rivers each year has declined, so in an attempt to improve the situation many coastal and rivermouth netting stations have been closed down. Most Highland rivers are owned wholly or partly by estates and they argue that rod income far outweighs what they received from the nets. This argument may carry some weight but after virtually bringing to an end a way of life carried out for over 150 years, there has not yet been any significant increase in the rod catches.

RADIOING FOR THE PONY, REAY FOREST ESTATE, SUTHERLAND.

Once the stag has been killed and gralloched it is the pony boy/man's job to arrive at the scene and take the carcase back to the larder. This is sometimes easier said than done, as he may be up to three or four miles away, patiently waiting at a predetermined landmark, unaware that the stalk is finished. Over the years therefore, signalling to the pony boy has been perfected to almost an art form. Fires were lit, flags raised, shirts taken off and waved, and mirrors reflected, to list a few. Today, things have improved, and they go to the hill equipped with radio transmitters. Of course they are not always able to use them because of bad weather or terrain interference, and I've still seen the odd shirt or scarf blowing in the wind.

99

SIGNALLING FOR THE PONY, REAY FOREST ESTATE, SUTHERLAND.

THE STALKER'S BURDEN, ACHNACARRY FOREST NORTH, LOCHEIL'S ESTATE, LOCHABER.
The stalker takes control out on the hill, directing operations and making the necessary decisions. He decides which stag the 'rifle' will go for, and the best way to go about it. No matter who he is escorting, it is his responsibility to ensure that the stag is killed as quickly and as painlessly as possible. In the event of it being wounded he would have to go after it. The stalker also has the responsibility of getting the carcase within reach of the pony or vehicle.

HOODWINKING A PONY, BEN ARMINE, SUTHERLAND.
This bizarre looking tactic, using the stalkers jacket, is occasionally employed to help calm the pony as a stag is lowered onto its back.

Loading The Pony, Reay Forest Estate, Sutherland.

BRINGING HOME A STAG HARRIS-STYLE, NORTH HARRIS ESTATE.
After it has been shot and gralloched, a stag is usually dragged down to a pony or loaded onto a vehicle, depending on access. On North Harris, in the Outer Hebrides, stalkers have devised their own time honoured method of getting stags down from their boulder-strewn mountainsides. I could hardly believe a man could walk with a 12 stone carcase strapped to his shoulders the two miles back to the vehicle.

STALKING CELEBRATION, SUISGILL ESTATE, SUTHERLAND.
After being dragged a few hundred yards through
heather, bog, and burns, the stag is unceremoniously
strapped to the back of the vehicle; then the stalking
party celebrates with a drink.

THE DUKE'S SHOOTING PARTY HEADING FOR ANOTHER
DRIVE, BLAIR CASTLE, PERTHSHIRE.

OPPOSITE
THE GHILLIES' BURDEN, LOCH VOSHMID, NORTH HARRIS
ESTATE.
Having spent all day skilfully manoeuvring the boat for
the fishermen, the ghillies then shoulder their load back
to the security of the lunch hut.

RETURNING HOME, REAY FOREST ESTATE, SUTHERLAND.
This coming-home procession was livened up by the foal, who refused to be left at the lodge, whilst Mum was off all day. It spent it's time trying to bite everybody, especially Nigger, the ghillie's labrador, and was banned from the next day's stalk.

THE END OF A DAY'S FISHING, GRIMERSTA, ISLE OF LEWIS.

BRINGING HOME A STAG, BEN ARMINE-STYLE, SUTHERLAND.
Throughout my estate visits I have seen all kinds of machines in operation, but this was the most memorable. It was being used by the ponyman, in preference to his pony, which he complained kept biting him. This power driven barrow had absolutely no suspension, with the result that every few yards it would tilt over as it hit a hummock or pothole, and the man would have to re-right it and replace the stag. By the end of the two mile trek back to Ben Armine he looked pretty flushed. It obviously hadn't bothered him though, for the next morning he opted to take the machine out again.

HAPPILY LEAVING THE RIVER, RIVER LAXFORD, SUTHERLAND.

THE LARDER, GOBERNUISGACH LODGE, REAY FOREST ESTATE, SUTHERLAND.
Lodge architecture varies quite dramatically from massive Scots Baronial piles to cramped corrugated iron shacks. However, deer larders whether in Sutherland, Argyll or the Outer Hebrides nearly always have the same kind of shape, with pagoda style roofs reminiscent of whisky distilleries.

THE POST MORTEM, THE LARDER, BEN ARMINE.
Once the deer carcase has reached the larder and is being skinned and butchered there is often an examination to see if it was a good 'shot', what damage was done, and what condition the animal was in. It is not uncommon, as in this case, that the stalker's children join the group and quite happily watch the examination. It's as much part of their home education, as would be that of the farmer's children who help with lambing.

THE GHILLIES' PERKS, REAY FOREST ESTATE, SUTHERLAND.
After the stalk, it has always been customary for the pony boys and ghillies to have the 'leftovers' from the lunch packs, liquid or solid. The amount they get, depends largely on just how good a day it's been, or how hard the 'rifle' thought they had worked.

OPPOSITE
NOT FORGETTING THE PONY, REAY FOREST ESTATE, SUTHERLAND.
Without fail, on every deer forest that I have visited, no matter what the weather conditions were, the ponies are groomed and fed as soon as they get back. I've seen deer saddles cleaned by stalkers soaked to the skin, who should have been straight home for a bath. These Highland ponies always seem to receive respect and affection from the hardest of men; sentiments not lavished on modern amphibious vehicles, which are dumped outside at night and hosed down in the morning.

THE CARNMORE STALKING PONIES, CARNMORE LODGE,
LETTEREWE WILDERNESS, WESTER ROSS.

The Grouse Larder, Invercauld Estate.

LABELLING THE DAY'S CATCH, GRIMERSTA, ISLE OF LEWIS.
This slab, on which they are labelling and preparing the day's catch for the freezer, was recently installed at Grimersta fishing lodge, to replace an older one. It is big enough to lay-out practically any catch caught today. One wonders how the old one coped with catches earlier this century, for it was common for a rod to catch double figures. In 1888, one man caught in a day, 54 salmon plus some sea trout, a British record which still holds.

OPPOSITE
THE SALMON SCALES, LOCHMORE LODGE.
If guests are fishing the river, it is customary on their return to the lodge to weigh-in the fish, record the catch details, and leave the fish on display. The details will be entered into an annual game book later. Many lodges have meticulous game books dating back to the beginning of the estate.

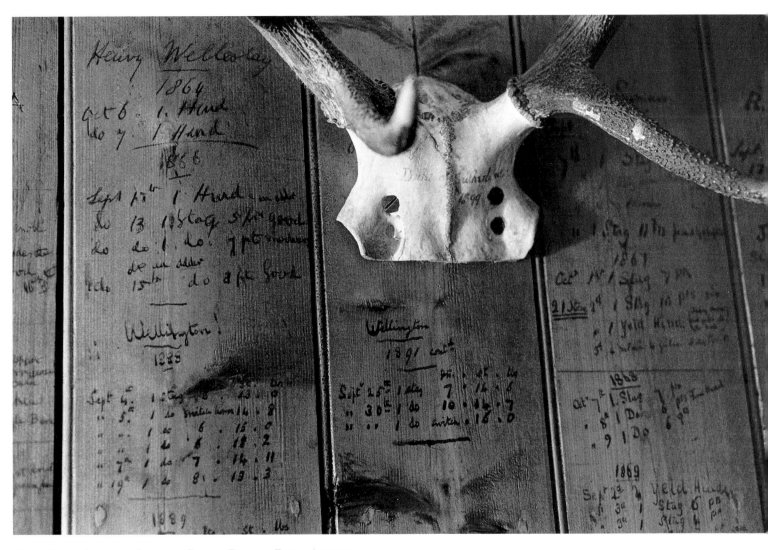

THE BEN ARMINE LODGE GAME BOOK, BEN ARMINE
ESTATE, SUTHERLAND.
At first glance the drawing room walls at Ben Armine
look like the work of some Victorian graffiti artist. The
etched and burnt scrawlings are in fact the old game
book featuring many celebrated names who stayed at
the lodge.

PREPARING A BATH, INVERCAULD HOUSE.
One of the daily high points of staying in an old lodge is taking a bath; particularly after coming off the hill drenched and cold. These cavernous tubs filled to the brim, often with dark peaty water, miraculously heal all aches and strains. After a soak the day's mishaps, such as dropping a camera into a burn, never seem quite as bad.

A Stalker's Dream, Langwell, Caithness.
This profusion of trophy heads is what most Victorian
stalkers dreamt of taking home with them. Nowadays,
the stalker contents himself with shooting the 'rubbish'
heads, leaving the trophies to breed.

AFTERNOON TEA AFTER A HARD DAY ON THE MOOR, THE TWELFTH OF AUGUST, CABRACH HOUSE, GLENFIDDICH ESTATE.
Like the bath, another welcome ritual at lodges is afternoon tea. Not always consumed in such grand settings, it is usually demolished with the same enthusiasm. The poor day's shooting may have dampened their first day's enthusiasm but not their appetite.

DONNY TAKES IN THE MATCH, SUISGILL KENNELS, SUTHERLAND.

Keepers laugh at the nine till five concept of work as they do the term 'regular week'. Outwith the routine of the season, jobs are fitted in when and where they can be, and throughout the winter and spring they can still be pretty busy. There are hinds to cull, kennels to maintain, vehicles to repair, deer to be fed, fencing to erect, heather burning, putting out grit for the grouse, vermin control and keeping an eye out for poachers. Jobs such as vermin control and poacher-watching often go on at night, so Donny is glad to have an opportunity to put his feet up and watch this midweek European Cup game. On this freezing February night his dogs too were taking advantage of the fire.

ALL IN A DAY'S WORK, SUISGILL KENNELS KITCHEN, SUTHERLAND.

As well as being kept busy with keepering activities Donny is hardly inactive in his spare time. It is not uncommon to walk into the Suisgill Kennels kitchen at six o'clock in the evening, and find a full-blown piping lesson in progress. Student pipers parade up and down while dogs take cover under chairs, and Norma, Donny's wife, tries to get dinner together, as well as chat to a waiting parent.

AFTER DINNER ENTERTAINMENT, INVERCAULD HOUSE.
The hospitality given to guests at Invercauld by Capt. Farquharson is unique. Most of the 'guests' are paying Americans who get to share breakfast, lunch and dinner with the Laird, if they wish. To enhance the atmosphere as dinner is ending, the clan Farquharson piper enters the candlelit room and plays as he encircles the dinner table. He then moves off, taking the guests with him, to an adjoining room where he plays traditional music for the next half hour as coffee and drinks are served.

THE GHILLIES BALL, LOCHMORE LODGE.
It has always been customary for estates to have an end of season celebration for the staff, given and attended by the owner, family and guests. The idea is to have a good old get-together which breaks down any social barriers for the evening. This one at Lochmore was no exception with Anne Duchess of Westminster, being burled centre left of photo, and Gerald, sixth Duke of Westminster and his wife, extreme right, all being grabbed by various estate employees, for dances until well after midnight. Unfortunately for employees on many estates, these gatherings have become a thing of the past. This particular one which I photographed in 1985, was to be the last at Lochmore Lodge. However it has been continued on a slightly smaller scale by the Duchess at her new residence on the estate.

AFTER THE SEASON IS OVER.
The following pictures were taken at a time of year when few people would dare venture out onto the Scottish hills let alone go to work. Keepers on estates with deer forests have a responsibility to cull red deer hinds between 20 October and 15 February, and therefore carry out this task during some of the worst winter weather.

SPYING FOR HINDS, KINGIE DEER FOREST, LOCHABER.

GOING TO WORK BY BOAT, KINGIE DEER FOREST.
At this time of year the only practicable means of getting to the hinds, for Alex Boyd and son Farquhar, is by crossing Loch Quoich. They are experienced boatmen since they use it most days during the stalking season.

PROTECTING THE BOAT, KINGIE DEER FOREST.
Farquhar continuously breaks surface ice in front of the boat to protect the bow. The previous week the boat had been holed by ice and they had to ram their waterproofs into the cut to ensure they got home. Very reassuring for passengers!

LOADING THE CULLED HINDS, KINGIE DEER FOREST.
Once out of the boat, Alex and Farquhar had a steepish
climb up to a ridge, but soon located a large group of
hinds. Before long they had hauled six dead hinds down
to the boat and loaded them. I sensed an urgency in
Alex, that I had not seen in a keeper before. As we
pushed off for the return journey it began to snow, and
the further into the loch we got the heavier it fell.

RETURNING HOME FROM HIND SHOOTING, KINGIE DEER FOREST.

As the snow increased, the boat's progress slowed but Farquhar kept up his ice breaking tactics regardless. The frozen loch surface merged with the whited-out landscape, and I'm sure Alex must have been guiding the boat by instinct, since I certainly couldn't make out a thing beyond Farquhar at the front. Eventually the grey form of their vehicle slowly began to emerge from the gloom, and we were there, frozen but safe. The typical photographer, I asked them to leave me ashore and go back out again and re-land (not really expecting they would oblige). Without hesitation, out they sailed once more then came back in and unloaded. I couldn't feel my fingers to focus, let alone see clearly through the viewfinder but I did snap a few frames, and this one I think communicates the feel of what it was like that day.

135

WINTERING STAG, LOCHABER.